Cracks
in the
Sidewalk

Children's Daily Adventures

Cracks in the Sidewalk

Children's Daily Adventures

by
Crystal Bowman

CYGNET PUBLISHING CO.
2153 Wealthy St. SE, #238
Grand Rapids, Michigan 49506

Contents

DAILY DISASTERS

IN MY ROOM

DEDICATION:

to Bob, Rob, Scott, and Teri, with love.

With special thanks to

Frank J. Hackinson
Alan G. Hartman
Nancy Faber and
Randall Faber

for making it possible.

Come with me and you will see
A world of sweet reality,
Where happiness and love are free,
And things are how they ought to be.
Sometimes tranquil, sometimes wild,
'Tis the world of an innocent child.

Little People

Why?

Why do cows make milk?
Why do bees make honey?
Why does rain fall from the sky?
Why are summers sunny?

Why do mice eat cheese?
Why do babies cry?
Why are zebras black and white?
Why do robins fly?

Why do cats have kittens?
Why do hens lay eggs?
Why do stars come out at night?
Why do flies have legs?

I have so many questions,
And often wonder, why?
I have a lot of things to learn;
I'm just a little guy.

No Such Thing

There's no such thing as monsters,
The sandman's make-believe.
Leprechauns are just a myth,
Intended to deceive.

Witches, ghosts, and goblins,
Don't scare me anymore.
Fairies, elves, and unicorns,
Are actually a bore.

I'm old enough to know that
These things are just pretend.
But please don't say a word to my
Imaginary friend.

Sit Still!

My father says to sit up straight,
My Mother says, "Don't squirm!"
They say that I remind them
Of a wiggle, wiggle worm.
My ankles get so tired
When they're hanging in the air.
They feel a whole lot better
When I rest them on my chair.
Sitting still in grown-up chairs
Is really quite a chore.
But life will be more pleasant
When my feet can touch the floor.

Success

I finally did it,
I'm so very proud!
I finally did it,
I'll shout it out loud!

Couldn't do it before
Though I tried and I tried.
And now I can do it,
I'm bursting with pride.

Let me tell you about
My very good news,
Today I learned how
To tie my own shoes!

Magic Wand

I have a pretty magic wand
With glitter on the end.
I've learned to use it wisely,
It's almost like a friend.
When my room is messy
And cleaning is a chore,
I wave my magic wand
And touch the toys upon the floor.
Then suddenly they come alive
And much to my surprise,
They quickly put themselves away
Before my very eyes.
Another trick I like to do
Is when it's time to eat,
I wave my wand across the food
So everything tastes sweet.
I turn my soup to ice cream
And eat it right away.
These magic tricks are wonderful!
I do them every day.
If you don't have a magic wand
Just find yourself a stick.
Use imagination,
And do a magic trick!

I Wish I Could Whistle!

I sure wish that I could whistle!
I practice everyday.
Everyone else can do it,
At least it seems that way.

Every time I try it,
I hold my lips just so.
I fill my mouth with lots of air,
And then I blow and blow.

But no, I never whistle,
I only blow lots of air.
Perhaps someday I will do it,
By then, I probably won't care.

A Picture for Mama

"Mama, I drew a nice picture for you.
Right there on the wall,
And I painted it too!
I drew all those flowers
And painted them green.
Isn't it truly a wonderful scene?
I made one for you
And I made one for me.
These pictures are beautiful,
Don't you agree?"
My mother just stood there
With tears in her eyes.
I could tell by her face
That she loved my surprise!

Someone Else's Birthday

It's someone else's birthday,
That's the way it always is.
The birthday party's never mine,
It's always hers or his.

I do like going to parties,
And playing birthday games.
But the letters on the birthday cake
Spell someone else's name.

My friend is so excited,
His birthday's almost here.
But I won't have a birthday
For at least another year.

That's why I'm so unhappy,
And feeling sad today.
You see, I had my birthday
Only yesterday.

Little Sister

I have a little sister
With curly golden hair.
I like to read her stories
And rock her in the chair.

She's so much fun to play with.
She's small and cute and funny.
She loves her teddy bear,
And her furry, yellow bunny.

I love my little sister.
I'm proud to be her brother,
But when she has a dirty pants
I bring her to my mother.

Friends and Neighbors

Where Are My Friends?

I'm walking up and down the street
Hoping that by chance I'll meet
Someone who will want to play
On this warm and sunny day.

It seems that no one is around,
One single friend cannot be found.
I guess I'll have to go back home,
Where I will sit and be alone.
But as I reach my house I see
My friends have come to play with me!

Gathered at my own front door
Are five or six or even more.
My friends have all come out to play
On this warm and sunny day.

Alan

Hello, my name is Alan,
And I would like to say,
I spell my name A-L-A-N
And that's the only way!

Some folks put in extra l's,
Some spell it with an E.
When people spell my name all wrong,
It really bothers me!

So if you want to be my friend,
I'll tell you one more time,
Please spell my name correctly,
And things will be just fine.

Charles

Charles had snarls all over his hair.
His hair was too long and he just didn't care.
He never took time for a brush or a comb,
His hair looked so bad that he had to stay home.
For when he went out, all the people would stare
At Charles with snarls all over his hair.

Then one day he went to a barber shop,
And he said to the barber, "These snarls must stop!"
The barber took scissors, a razor, and cream.
Then he cut and he shaved 'til his head was all clean.
Then Charles got up and he walked out the door,
While his snarls lay still on the barber shop floor.

Now when he goes out the people still stare.
His snarls are gone, and so is his hair.

Messy Bess

I had a friend named messy Bess,
Whose bedroom always was a mess.
She never ever made her bed,
Nor put away the books she read.
She never put her clothes away,
But left them on the floor to stay.

Her toys were scattered everywhere,
And dolls were piled on her chair.
Her mom and dad did all they could
To make her change. It did no good.
She always kept her room a mess.
That's why we called her
   messy Bess.

But then the circus came to town,
With acrobats and a silly clown.
Her family went to see the show,
But messy Bess, she could not go.
She couldn't find her coat or shoes,
Or the money she had planned to use.
When everybody said good bye,
Messy Bess began to cry.

She learned a lesson on that day,
And put her clothes and shoes away.
She cleaned her room and made her bed,
And put away the books she read.
Well, since that day her room's been clean,
So now we call her clean Marlene.

Marilyn May and Mike

I know of a girl named Marilyn May
Who has a brother named Mike.
The problem is, that Marilyn May
And her brother look almost alike.
And they get so upset if you get their names wrong,
And you can't tell the one from the other.
But I never quite know if it's Marilyn May,
Or if it's maybe her brother.
Each time I see them I'm very confused,
And I really don't know what to say.
So instead of getting them very upset,
I usually just walk away.
Well, I've finally found a solution
For these siblings who look just alike.
From now on, if I should meet one of them,
I'll just call it Marilyn Mike.

Walter

Why did they name me Walter?
I wish it were Peter or Paul.
I wish it were Scott or Samuel;
Walter's the worst name of all.

It could have been Bobby or Billy,
Or Johnny, Jason or Jim.
It could have been Ryan or Robby,
Or Tommy, Terry, or Tim.

Oh, why did they name me Walter?
I'd like to be Danny or Don.
I'd like to be Michael or Marcus,
Or Reggie, Randy, or Ron.

Oh, why did they name me Walter?
It's the very worst name in the world.
I hate to complain at the sound of a name,
But, you see, it's because I'm a girl!

Friends

A friend is someone who listens,
A friend is someone who cares.
A friend is someone who understands,
A friend is someone who shares.

It's nice to have a special friend
To tell all your secrets to.
It's nice to know that someone you like,
Is someone who really likes you.

A friend is someone you call on the phone
To talk about nothing at all.
A friend is someone who cheers you up,
And makes you feel ten feet tall.

Everyone would like to have
A special friend it's true.
But if you want a special friend,
You need to be one, too.

Tinkerton

Have you ever heard of a Tinkerton?
Do you think that you know what it is?
Do you think it's something that glows in the dark,
Or something that maybe goes "fizz"?

Perhaps you may think it's an animal,
Or something from outer space.
Or maybe you think that a Tinkerton
Is just a far away place.

Well, a Tinkerton isn't an animal,
And it isn't a space ship or toy.
And a Tinkerton isn't a far away place,
A Tinkerton's simply a boy.

And if you're wondering how I know,
You may think it is really a shame,
When I tell you that the word Tinkerton,
Happens to be my first name!

School Days

School Days

On Monday, I wish I could watch T.V.,
But I have to go to school.

On Tuesday, I'd love to swim in the sea,
But I have to go to school.

On Wednesday, I'd like to ride my bike,
But I have to go to school.

On Thursday, I wish I could go for a hike,
But I have to go to school.

On Friday, I'd love to go to the zoo,
But I have to go to school.

On Saturday, there's not a thing to do,
I wish I could go to school.

My Lunch Box

When I come in from recess
I'm as hungry as a bear.
I open up my lunch box
And sit down on my chair.

First, I eat my cookie,
Then I eat my chips.
Then I use my napkin
To wipe my salty lips.

Next, I eat my apple,
My mother says I must.
I finally eat my sandwich,
But I never eat my crust.

$25x$

$x^2 +$

$2x +$

$x^2 +$

Algebra

I've always liked arithmetic,
I think that it is great.
Two plus two adds up to four,
And four plus four is eight.
But now I'm learning algebra
And I am so perplexed!

Somehow three plus twenty-nine,
Is Y or Z or X!
I don't like adding letters,
Letters are for words.
I'd rather work with numbers.
This math is for the birds!

$$6x^2 - 7x =$$
$$ax + bx + c =$$

Plurals!

One is a goose,
And two are called geese.
But two little mouses,
Are never called meese!

Two are called dice,
But one is a die,
And two octopuses
Are called octopi.

One is a knife.
And two are called knives.
One is a wife,
And two are called wives.

But, one is a deer
And two are called deer.
These plurals are very
Confusing, I fear!

Two little fishes
Are sometimes called fish,
But sometimes they're fishes.

Oh, how I wish
That to make all words plural,
You just add an "s".
But that is not the rule
And so I just guess!

The Play

I have a very important part
In the fifth-grade Christmas play.
I've practiced and I've memorized
The words I'm going to say.

I have the most important part,
I've got to get it right.
Perhaps I'll be a famous star
On center stage tonight.

I'm just a little nervous,
In fact, I'm really scared!
That's why I've practiced and rehearsed,
I need to be prepared.

I think I'll practice one more time,
Let's see, it goes like this:
"Thanks for coming here tonight,
Now you are dismissed."

Tuna Sandwich

I got my brother's sandwich
In my lunch box by mistake.
This one smells like tuna fish,
It's not the kind I take.
I cleared my throat politely,
I raised my hand and said,
"Would anybody like to trade
For tuna fish on bread?"

Freddie took my sandwich
And gave me chocolate cake.
Maybe there are just a few more
Trades that I can make.
"Would anybody like to have
This piece of colby cheese?"
Katie said, "I'll eat it!"
So I said, "Take it, please!"

She gave me her potato chips
And oatmeal cookie, too.
Perhaps I'll make another trade
Before this lunch is through.
I gave away my apple
For a brownie and some gum.
I never knew that eating lunch
At school could be such fun.

My lunch was so delicious,
I savored every bite.
The brownie and the cookie
Were truly a delight!
I ate all my potato chips
And Freddie's chocolate cake.
My brother's tuna sandwich
Was a wonderful mistake!

My Paper Monster

Oh, his legs look like spaghetti
And his nose is round and green.
He has got the most enormous eyes
That you have ever seen.
He is ugly, he is scary,
That is why I love him so.
He's my very own creation
And I'm proud to tell you so.
He's my awesome paper monster
That I made at school today.
And he's going to be so helpful
'Cause he'll chase the girls away.
I'll put him by my bedroom door
To keep my sister out.
As soon as she encounters him,
I know she'll scream and shout.
Oh, I know he'll cause excitement
Like I've never seen before.
He is such a great creation,
I think I'll make some more!

An Apple a Day

The Shot

I have to go and have a shot,
For some disease I haven't got.
It makes no sense at all to me
To put myself through misery.

I'm healthy, strong, and feeling fine.
In two more weeks I'm turning nine.
I do not want to have a shot
For some disease I haven't got.

Allergies

Get that cat
Away from me, please.
He's coming too close
And he's making me sneeze.

Don't bring me flowers
When I'm sick in bed.
They stuff up my nose
And they clog up my head.

When I eat peanuts,
Or candy, or cheese,
I break out in hives
And I cough and I wheeze.

Wool makes me itch,
So I can't wear a sweater.
Without all my allergies,
Life would be better!

Vitamins

I must take my vitamins A, B, and C.
'Cause vitamins are very good for me.
A helps my ankles,
B strengthens my back.
C helps my collar bone, so it won't crack.
D feeds my brain, so I won't be dumb.
E gives me energy, to help me run.
F makes me fast,
G makes me feel great.
H makes me happy, I hardly can wait!
By taking my vitamins, that's what I get.
So give me a dose of the whole alphabet!

Chicken Pox

Oh, look at all my horrid spots!
I think I've got the chicken pox.
They're on my arms and on my nose.
They're even in between my toes.
They're on my chest and in my hair,
These chicken pox are everywhere!
They're on my feet and elbows, too.
I don't know what I'm going to do.
Twelve new spots appeared today.
I wish that they would go away,
So I could go outside to play.

Chocolate Medicine

Chocolate flavored medicine
Would taste so very good!
I know I'd gladly take it
If my mother said I should.
I would not make a face,
Or close my mouth, or turn my head.
I would not cause a fuss
Or go and hide beneath my bed.
If I had chocolate medicine,
I know I'd love the taste.
I'd finish every single drop,
It would not go to waste.
If I was ever feeling sick,
I'd take it right away.
And then I'd feel so good
That I would go outside to play.
Chocolate flavored medicine
Would never spoil or mold.
Will someone please invent it
Before I get too old?

Loose Tooth

My tooth came loose
The other day.
It happened while I was at play.
I wiggled it
With all my might,
Back and forth,
Left and right.

Then all of a sudden,
Out it came.
A little blood,
A little pain.
And now I have a little hole.
It's where my tongue
Just seems to go.

The Singing Dentist

I really like my dentist
Except for just one thing.
Every time I visit him,
He always starts to sing.

A week ago last Monday—
And I'm telling you the truth,
He sang "Don't Ever Leave Me,"
While he pulled my wisdom tooth.

If you have a favorite song,
Just ask him and he will
Sing most any lyric
To the rhythm of his drill.

And if he doesn't know the words,
He'll just make up his own.
Sometimes he is so silly
That I roll my eyes and groan!

I really like my dentist,
And it wouldn't bother me
To hear his constant singing
If he learned to sing on key!

If You Don't

If you don't brush your teeth
They will surely fall out.

If you don't wash your face
You'll get pimples no doubt.

If you don't take a bath
You may get some disease.

If you don't blow your nose,
You will probably sneeze.

If you don't clean your toes
They will maybe fall off.

If you don't wear your coat
You will get a bad cough.

If you don't eat your meat
You may never be strong.

So do all of this
And you'll never go wrong.

In the Kitchen

Cereal

Cereal is the very best food
That you could ever eat.
It's better than fruit or vegetables,
And certainly better than meat.

I wish I could eat it three times a day,
Every day of the year.
If I could be granted this simple request,
I'd dance on my tiptoes and cheer!

I love the kind with raisins and nuts,
And the kind that has sugary flakes.
I like the way it floats in my milk,
And the sound that cereal makes.

Sometimes I sneak it when no one's around.
I'm truly as sly as a fox.
But the kind I like best, above all the rest,
Is the kind with a prize in the box!

Peanut Butter Sandwich

In the pantry in our kitchen
There is food on every shelf.
There's a snack that I enjoy,
And I can get it by myself.

When I'm feeling hungry
And I need to fill my belly,
I find the peanut butter,
Get some bread and lots of jelly.

Then I make a tasty sandwich,
And I gobble every bite.
A peanut butter sandwich
Is simply a delight.

You can eat your cold bologna
Or enjoy some ham and cheese.
But for me, when I am hungry
I say, "Peanut butter, please!"

Pizza Time

Pepperoni, sauce and cheese,
May I have some pizza, please?
Chewy crusts are extra nice,
May I have another slice?

Who's that other pizza for?
May I have a little more?
Six more pieces then I'll stop,
Wash it down with soda pop.

Feeling just a little stuffed,
I think that I have had enough.
Pepperoni, sauce and cheese,
No more pizza for me, please!

Vegetables

Vegetables are the most horrible food,
I am really sorry to say!
My mother thinks I should eat some of them
Seven or eight times a day.

Spinach is soggy and smells like wet grass,
And I think that it comes from the sea.
Cabbage is fine for my mother and dad,
But it tastes awfully sour to me.

Beans can be yellow, or they can be green,
Broccoli looks like a tree.
Whatever the color or size or shape,
It certainly doesn't please me.

I do try to eat my vegetables,
But the ones I especially hate,
I put on my fork and I hide every piece
Beneath the edge of my plate.

Don't blame me for not liking vegetables,
It really isn't my fault.
I'm sure whoever invented them,
Must have been an adult.

Bug in My Stew

I was eating my stew
Then decided to stop,
'Cause a bug was floating
Right there on the top.
I didn't get frightened
Or let out a shout,
I simply decided
To get the bug out.

The stew was delicious
I have to admit,
It tasted so good
That I ate quite a bit.
I finally finished
And there in my mug,
Way at the bottom
I saw one more bug.

I could have been angry,
I could have been sad,
But the stew was the best
That I ever had!
So when you are making
A flavorful stew,
Remember to throw in
A small bug or two.

Gingerbread Man

Once I made a gingerbread man.
I rolled him out and put him in a pan.
I put some candy on his face,
Oh, how delicious he will taste!
I put some raisins on his chest.
Buttons for his tiny vest.
I put him in the oven to bake,
What a yummy treat he'll make.

I took him out when he was done,
Eating him will be such fun!
I picked him up, I couldn't wait,
But then I put him on the plate.
He looked at me as if to say,
"Please, don't eat me up today!"
I smiled at him and shook my head.
I ate a candy bar instead.

Mother and Grandma

My mother feeds me tuna fish
With broccoli on the side.
But Grandma gives me candy
When my mouth is open wide.
My mother slices apples
And oranges for dessert.
My grandma brings me doughnuts
If she finds out I am hurt.

My mother makes me drink my milk
Most every single night.
But Grandma gives me ice cream bars
When I do something right.
My mother cooks up rice and beans
That have an awful taste.
So I say, "See ya later,
I'm going to Grandma's place!"

Baker's Blues

I tried to bake some cookies,
But I left them in too long.
I tried to bake a chocolate cake,
But everything went wrong!

I tried to make some brownies,
But I dropped them on the floor.
I think I'll stop this baking
And start heading for the store.

Daily Disasters

Cracks in the Sidewalk

My brother said be careful,
My sister said beware.
When you're walking on the sidewalk
You'd better walk with care.
You'd better pay attention
And listen to these facts,
'Cause your life will be in danger
If you step on any cracks.

You just might cause an earthquake,
Or fall upon your nose.
When you're walking on the sidewalk
You'd better watch your toes.
And if you see a big one
That's long and deep and wide,
You'd better step on over
Or you'll tumble down inside.

And then you'll go to China
Or maybe to Peru.
The cracks upon the sidewalk
Could be the end of you!
I listened to my sister
And I listened to my brother.
They really had me frightened,
So I went and told my mother.

Tree House

I built a nifty tree house
In a lovely maple tree.
I fell out of my tree house,
Broke my arm and skinned my knee.

I built another tree house
From some lumber that I found.
My second nifty tree house,
Is much closer to the ground.

Mosquito Bite

Is there anyone out there
Who happens to know
How to get this mosquito bite
Off of my toe?

It itches and itches
And drives me berserk!
I've tried lots of remedies;
None of them work.

I wrapped it with tissue
And used special lotion.
My grandmother mixed up
Mosquito bite potion.

But still, it just itches
From morning 'til night.
My life's been disrupted
With this little bite!

Roller Skates

Oh, my goodness sakes!
I'm wearing roller skates,
And I'm feeling mighty shaky inside.

My feet don't seem to know
Where they're supposed to go,
So I think it's going to be a short ride!

My New Pet

I found him on the sidewalk,
He was cold and scared and wet.
I held him in my arms,
And took him home to be my pet.
I washed him in the bathtub,
Things were going very well.

Then my mother came and asked me
Why she sensed a funny smell.
When she saw my little critter,
She fell down with a thunk.
Do you think that I should ask her
If she'll let me keep my skunk?

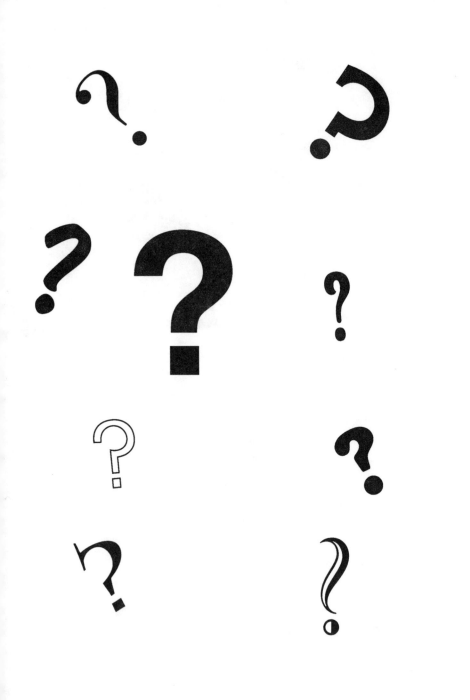

Forgetful Blues

I forgot to do my homework,
I forgot to tie my shoes.
I forgot to call my mother,
I forgot to pay my dues.
I forgot my lunch on Friday,
I forgot to do my chores.
I forgot to wear my jacket,
When I went to play outdoors.

I forgot to mail a letter,
I forgot to mow the lawn.
I forgot to say, "Excuse me,"
When I had a giant yawn.
I forgot to feed my goldfish,
I forgot to make my bed.
And now I know the problem,
I forgot to use my head.

Looking and Looking

Will somebody help me?
I'm loosing my mind!
I'm looking for something
I simply can't find.

I know that I put it
Right over there.
And now I can't find it,
It's not anywhere.

I've looked by the window,
Behind every door,
I've looked in the closet,
And searched every drawer.

It's not in the corners,
Nor under my bed.
I'm truly convinced
That I'm loosing my head.

Hey, wait just a minute,
Isn't it grand?
Nothing is missing,
It's in my left hand!

Why Do I Laugh?

Why do I laugh, I do not know,
When my little sister stubs her toe?
Why do I howl and roll on the floor
When my mother walks into the bathroom door?
Why do I chuckle and cover my face

When my brother trips over his tennis shoe lace?
Why do I giggle and hide in my bed
When my father stoops over and bumps his head?
Hey, wait a minute, stop laughing at me!
I fell off a chair and skinned my knee!

Ink on My Finger

There's ink on my finger,
Oh, what should I do?
If I don't get it off,
All my skin will turn blue.

I'll be blue forever,
For twenty-one years.
I knew this would happen,
It was one of my fears.

I'd better do something
To help right away,
Or I will be blue
By the end of the day.

I could try some water,
Or maybe some soap.
If this doesn't work,
There will be no more hope.

I'd better act quickly,
I'd better not linger.
There must be a way
To get ink off my finger.

I Swallowed My Gum

I feel so dumb, I swallowed my gum!
I wonder where it will go.
Will it keep going down as I jump all around?
Will it stop at the end of my toe?
The thought of it all just makes me quiver!
Oh, what am I going to do?

It could get stuck on my ribs or my liver,
Or maybe I'll get the flu.
Should I call a doctor or look for my mom,
Or maybe go find the police?
While I contemplate upon my fate,
I think I'll have another piece.

The Bubble

I blew a great big bubble
While chewing gum today.
It stretched out wide before it popped,
I'm really pleased to say.
A little gum got on my cheeks,
And in my nose and hair.
My eyebrows felt a little weird,
But I didn't really care.

My ears were just a little plugged,
Some gum was on my chin.
The collar of my oxford shirt
Was sticking to my skin.
The bubble was enormous,
The noise was very loud.
My mother wasn't happy,
But I was very proud!

No Fair

My parents get to stay up late to watch a T.V. show,
But if I ask to join them, of course, they answer no!
They get to use the telephone most any time at all.
But I must ask permission before I make a call.
My father gets to have dessert before he eats his meat.
But I must finish all my food before I get a treat.
If Mother's room is messy, she simply shuts the door.
But I loose my allowance if my clothes are on the floor.

When Father belches loudly, he blames it on the food.
But if I make a little noise, they say I'm being rude.
My mother gets to use the car when she goes here or there,
But I must walk or ride my bike, it simply isn't fair!
My parents just came home from work, they've had a
    tiresome day.
While they prepare my dinner, I'm going outside to play.

The Tiny Bumblebee

I saw a tiny bumblebee
Just buzzin' through the air.
The bumblebee was not aware
That I was standing there.
So I began to chase him
'Til he landed on a wall.
He looked so scared and helpless,
I was not afraid at all.
But then it seemed he noticed me,
And followed me around.

I quickly tried to run away,
But stumbled to the ground.
And then, that tiny bumblebee,
He did a nasty thing;
He sat upon my forehead,
And gave me quite a sting!
This tragic little incident
Has made me very wise.
I've learned that I must never judge
Another by its size.

Hiccups

I had a case of hiccups,
Just the other day.
I tried most every remedy,
To make them go away.

I drank a glass of water,
I drank a glass of pop.
I held my breath
   'til I was blue,
But still, they did not stop.

I turned around in circles,
And on my head I stood.
I even tried to scare myself,
But still, it did no good.

I couldn't stop my hiccups so
I went outside to play.
When I forgot I had them,
My hiccups went away.

Heebee Jeebees

Please don't scratch the chalkboard,
I just don't like that sound.
It gives me heebee jeebees,
And my skin crawls up and down.

When you eat your dinner,
Please don't scrape your plate.
I get the heebee jeebees
When I hear sounds I hate.

The heebee jeebees get me
When I see things I dread,
Like roaches in the closet,
And spiders in my bed.

I get the heebee jeebees,
I shiver, shake, and squirm,
When deep inside my apple
I find a tiny worm.

Listen to me, children,
This warning is for you:
Be careful what your see and hear,
Or they may get you too!

In My Room

Which Side?

One day when I was grumpy,
My mother smiled and said,
"You got up this morning,
On the wrong side of your bed."

Ever since that day,
I've tried to figure out,
Which side I should get in,
And which side I should get out.

So sometimes when I'm grumpy,
And it's not a pleasant day,
I jump back into bed,
And get out a different way.

Beneath My Bed

I do not like to go to bed
And lie there for a while,
Because I know a crocodile,
Who has a large, suspicious smile,
Lives underneath my bed.
I almost want to scream and shout
When Father turns the hall light out,
Because I know the snakes come out
From underneath my bed.

I don't dare move, I lie so still,
Because I know the monsters will
Sit upon my window sill.
They're underneath my bed.
I fall asleep though anyway,
And wake up with the light of day.
The creatures all have gone away,
Back beneath my bed.

My Room

I hate to clean my bedroom,
But my mother says I must.
She doesn't like the messy floor,
The fingerprints, or dust.

I think it's quite attractive
With an interesting decor.
I've piled all my dirty clothes
So neatly on the floor.

My soccer ball and baseball
Are much easier to find,
Sitting on my windowsill,
Beneath my mini blind.

The candy wrappers on my desk
Are really not that old.
The pop cans on my bookshelf
Look great with all that mold.

The cobwebs do not bother me,
In fact, I think they're nice.
The cookie crumbs beneath my bed
Have helped to feed the mice.

I like collecting magazines,
I need one hundred more.
It only takes a day or two
To close my closet door.

I'm very safe and comfortable
Within my private room.
I think I'll stay for twenty years,
And never use a broom.

Bedtime

One thing that I really dread
Is when I have to go to bed.
Especially when I'm wide awake—
It makes no sense for goodness' sake!
Then after counting ninety sheep,
I close my eyes and fall asleep.

Then Mother comes to wake me up.
(She sometimes has to shake me up!)
But I would rather stay in bed—
It makes no sense, just like I said!
I think that I should sleep all day,
'Cause nighttime is the time to play.

And Don't Forget to Say Your Prayers!

Dear God, I know you're with me
No matter where I go.
And I should never be afraid,
My mama told me so.

But when it's time to go to bed,
And Dad turns out the light,
It makes me very glad to know
That You stay up all night!

About the Author

Crystal Bowman is a homemaker, lyricist, and free-lance writer. She especially enjoys writing for children, and draws from her experience as a mother and former school teacher. When Crystal began sharing her poems with elementary and middle school students, the response was so positive that she wanted to make her poems available to the students. With the help of her illustrator, Crystal has created a delightful book that children of all ages and backgrounds will enjoy.

About the Illustrator

Aaron Williams developed an interest in art at an early age. His artistic abilities were recognized and encouraged during his elementary and middle school years. Aaron has the unique ability to combine humor with precise detail to create refreshingly individual illustrations. Aaron illustrated *Cracks in the Sidewalk* at the age of fourteen. He anticipates many more opportunities to use his artistic abilities in the future.